CRAZY CARS

by Matt Doeden

Jan Lahtonen, consultant and safety engineer, auto mechanic, and lifelong automobile enthusiast

Lerner Publications Company • Minneapolis

Cover Photo: Dave Major of Benton, Kansas, built this outrageous art car. The car itself is a BMW Isetta minicar. Major gave the car wings, a front propeller, a tailfin, and a name: Aero Car. (The car does not fly, however.)

Lerner Publications Company
A division of Lerner Publishing Group
241 First Avenue North
Minneapolis, MN 55401 U.S.A.

Website address: www.lernerbooks.com

Library of Congress Cataloging-in-Publication Data

Doeden, Matt.
    Crazy cars / by Matt Doeden.
        p.   cm. — (Motor mania)
    Includes bibliographical references and index.
    ISBN-13: 978–0–8225–6565–9 (lib. bdg. : alk. paper)
    ISBN-10: 0–8225–6565–X (lib. bdg. : alk. paper)
    1. Experimental automobiles—Juvenile literature. 2. Automobiles—Technological innovations—Juvenile literature. I. Title.
    TL147.D635 2007
    629.222—dc22   2006019400

Manufactured in the United States of America
1 2 3 4 5 6 – DP – 12 11 10 09 08 07

Contents

For more than one hundred years, people have been building, driving, and dreaming of cars. In the late 1800s, inventors began building the first "horseless carriages." Since then, cars have always represented freedom and possibilities. Many people dream of fast sports cars, expensive luxury cars, or powerful trucks. Others have a great deal more imagination. These are the people who build unusual cars. These strange machines look nothing like the cars we're used to seeing.

Crazy cars have been around for as long as automobiles have existed. But what exactly is a crazy car? For this book, a crazy car is any vehicle with new or weird shapes and features. Some are experiments. They are the result of people trying something new and different. Some were built just to be shocking or funny—or to get in the news. Still other crazy cars have been built to drive on roads *and* float on the water. Or fly through the air. Or get their power from the Sun. The possibilities are limited only by peoples' imaginations.

Chapter One

CRAZY CAR HISTORY

The earliest cars were hand built, one by one, and very expensive. The peculiar machines were seen as toys for the rich.

Before automobiles appeared in the late 1800s, people didn't have many options for traveling on land. Trains could carry them across long distances, but they could only go where rail lines could take them. People who wanted to go off on their own used horses. But all of that changed with the invention of the horseless carriage.

In some ways, all early automobiles could be called crazy cars. In the 1890s, the car was a new idea. No one had a fixed idea of what a car should look like or how it should work. The first car builders were inventors. They worked with their imaginations and the parts they had on hand.

Henry Ford proudly displays his very first working automobile, the *Quadricycle*. Ford built this very simple car in a brick shed behind his home. Ford would later go on to found the Ford Motor Company and become one of the world's richest men.

A Team Effort

The *Dunkley Moke*, built in the late 1800s, is one of the weirdest cars ever made. The car carried two passengers. The passengers faced in opposite directions. The front passenger controlled the steering, while the passenger in the rear controlled the brakes.

As a result, each car was a kind of experiment. Some early cars were little more than wagons with engines. Others were like Henry Ford's *Quadricycle*. Ford's first car was a simple frame with a gas-powered engine and four bicycle wheels mounted on it.

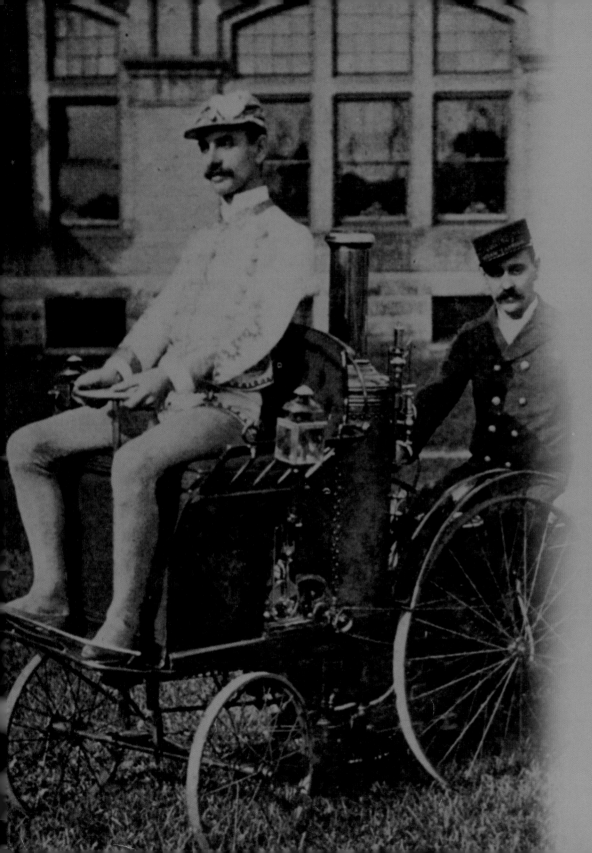

The Beginning

In the 1890s, most people thought cars were a crazy idea. The idea of getting around on roads without a horse or other animal seemed strange.

The first gasoline-powered cars weren't easy to start. A person had to turn a crank to get the engine to start. Once the machine did sputter to life, it was noisy. The engine smelled of gasoline fumes and exhaust. Most early cars were not very well built. They tended to break down often.

The first cars weren't easy to drive either. Speed limits and traffic laws didn't exist. Inexperienced drivers often got into accidents. They ran over sidewalks and sometimes people. They smashed into things. The noisy, smelly machines also scared horses.

Gasoline was not always the fuel of choice in the automobile's early days. *The Philion Road Carriage* (built in the early 1890s) burned coal and, later, oil.

At the time, many people thought of cars as a nuisance. Some wanted them outlawed altogether. But the new technology wasn't going away. People—and their horses—would have to get used to the sounds and smells of the horseless carriage.

In 1899 Uriah Smith came up with what he believed would be a solution to the problem. He built a car with a front end shaped like a horse. He named the car the Horsey Horseless. Smith hoped that its shape would comfort the horses that shared the road with it.

Smith wasn't the only person who dreamed of a car shaped like an animal. In 1912 R. N. Matthewson had a car built to look like a swan. But he didn't stop there. He also wanted it to *sound* like a swan. Matthewson had an organ placed inside the car that could make hissing noises, just like a real swan.

Smith and Matthewson weren't alone. The early 1900s were filled with strange cars. People still didn't have a

The Reeves Octoauto was one of the wildest car designs of the 1910s. The eight wheels were supposed to provide a smoother ride. But the car was too long and heavy to be practical.

clear idea of just how a car should look. Inventors kept experimenting with new shapes and ideas. One popular variation was the three-wheeled car. The German-built Gasi was one such car. It included seats for two riders. One rider sat in front of the other. Strangely, the Gasi's driver sat in the back seat, behind the passenger. Another odd three-wheeler was the Bow-V-Car of England. It was made mainly of plywood.

Some builders went the opposite direction. They added more wheels to their cars. The Reeves Octoauto had eight wheels, while the Sextoauto ran on six wheels. The builder, Milton Othello Reeves, thought that extra wheels would make for a smoother ride.

Other builders went with four wheels but arranged them in new ways. Some cars had their wheels placed in a diamond pattern. They had one wheel in front, one in back, and one on each side of the car near the middle. In the end, though, most people agreed that the best setup for a car was to have four wheels—two in the front and two in the back.

Model T Ford

Henry Ford's Ford Motor Company changed both cars and the car industry forever when he began building the Model T Ford in 1908. Ford used the first assembly line to build the cars. Each worker had a small, specific job. Together, they were able to turn out cars by the thousands. The Model T became the standard for how people thought a car should look.

Designers of the 1922 Reese Aerocar had seen how propellers pushed airplanes through the air at great speeds. They thought the idea might work for cars as well. So they mounted a big propeller to the back of the car. Combined with a small engine, the propeller actually gave the Aerocar a top speed of about 60 miles (96 km) per hour. But the car was slow to accelerate (speed up) and had poor handling, so the idea never took off.

Standing Out from the Crowd

By the 1930s, the car industry had changed. Most cars had the same basic design and shape. Individual inventors didn't have a place in the car industry anymore. Instead, large, organized companies such as General Motors (GM), Ford, and Chrysler, ruled the scene. These companies focused on building cars that would sell in large numbers. They weren't looking for radical ideas.

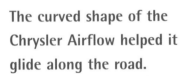

The curved shape of the Chrysler Airflow helped it glide along the road.

But a few unusual machines did come out of this period. One was the Chrysler Airflow. Introduced in 1934, the car was ahead of its time in many ways. It had a very smooth, flowing shape. It looked quite different from the big, bulky cars of the period. This shape made the Airflow very aerodynamic. It cut through the air easily. This helped make the car very fuel efficient. But the public did not like the Airflow's odd look. The car was a sales failure.

Another unusual car of the time was the Buick *Y-Job*. Built by GM in 1938, the car was also ahead of its time. It was low, long, and very stylish. Like the Airflow, it had an aerodynamic shape. The *Y-Job* also had many features that showed up on other GM cars in later years, including hidden headlights that swiveled out of view when turned off. The *Y-Job* also had a convertible roof that opened and closed with the touch of a button. This was a big advance from hand-cranked convertible tops.

General Motors chief designer Harley Earl sits in one of his proudest creations—the sleek and cutting-edge Buick *Y-Job*.

Minicars were in demand after World War II (1939–1945), especially in Europe. The continent's war-torn nations suffered through years of fuel shortages. These small, highly fuel-efficient cars allowed people to travel cheaply.

The *Y-Job* was truly one of a kind. In fact, GM built just one. The *Y-Job* turned out to be the very first concept car. Concept cars are idea cars. Most of them aren't built for mass production. They are experiments. Automakers build concept cars to test new shapes and designs.

Another trend that grew popular during the late 1930s and early 1940s was cars shaped to look like products. These productmobiles were just big, rolling advertisements. The cars took on shapes of food, candy bars, shoes, houses, and even bowling pins. The most famous productmobile was the

Oscar Mayer™ Wienermobile. It was shaped like—you guessed it—a giant hot dog.

Moving Forward

Many car lovers think of the 1950s as the golden age of automobiles. Dozens of models from that period have become classics and collector's items. But some cars from the 1950s have become memorable for their wackiness.

Minicars were one trend of the 1950s. These small cars often didn't run on gas. Some were electric powered. Many had only three wheels. Minicars were designed to be low priced and fuel efficient. They were sold mainly to families wanting a second car. Minicars didn't have the power or comfort of larger cars. Still, automakers hoped they would catch on. Models such as the AC Petite, the Gordon, and the Meyra enjoyed brief popularity. But in the end, the public rejected the minicar idea.

It's a Car, It's a Plane!

During the late 1940s, Washington State native Molt Taylor decided that cars should be able to fly. So he built the Aerocar. This small car towed a trailer that contained parts to turn the car into an airplane, including long wings and a tail. While the Aerocar could fly, it wasn't a very good plane or a very good car. Taylor built only five of them.

Firebird III (above) was the wildest Firebird yet. The titanium-bodied car had seven wings and tailfins. The 3/8-scale (3/8 the size of a normal car) model Ford *Nucleon (below)* was an experiment in what a nuclear-powered car might look like.

Meanwhile, the 1950s were the heyday of the concept car. Some of the world's craziest cars came out of the minds of concept car designers. Some, such as the 1958 Ford *Nucleon*, were never meant to actually run. Designers imagined the *Nucleon* as running on nuclear power. But building a nuclear reactor (engine) small enough to fit inside a car would have been impossible at the time. Still, the *Nucleon* got people thinking about how cars might look and work in the future. The Ford *X-1000*, meanwhile, looked so futuristic that some believed it could fly.

Other innovations were more practical. The GM Firebird series had a fantastic rocket-ship shape, but it also introduced useful ideas. The Firebird included new features such as electric windows and air conditioning. Designers also experimented with powerful gas turbine engines, similar to the kind found on jet aircraft. The Firebird represented style and speed. The most famous stock-car race in the world, the Daytona 500, even uses the Firebird's shape on the winner's trophy.

Full Custom

The 1950s and 1960s saw another big

car craze—customizing. People customized, or changed, their regular mass-produced cars into one-of-a-kind machines. Hot-rodders souped up their cars for racing. Others focused on making their cars look unique. The results were often spectacular machines, with strange shapes, multiple engines, and wild paint jobs.

Lowriders are a special kind of custom car. Their bodies can be lowered to ride close to the ground. It's a cool look that first came out of the Mexican American community of southern California. Most lowriders have a hydraulic system that raises and lowers the car. Some of these systems are so powerful that they can make the car jump several feet in the air. Another hallmark of lowriders are vivid paint schemes and shiny chrome and gold plating.

Recent Years

The 1970s saw many changes in the car industry. The Middle East oil

producers lowered oil output. This led to a major oil shortage in the United States, which bought most of its gas from the region. At the same time, the U.S. Congress passed laws that called for more fuel-efficient cars. Smaller cars became common in the 1970s. They included the compact Chevrolet Vega and the Ford Pinto.

Europeans responded to the gasoline shortage with even smaller cars. France's Acoma Super Comtesse had three wheels and a moped (small motorcycle) engine. Italy's Casalini Sulky had a similar design. The strangest of them all may have been the Flipper.

Above: Lowriders show off their cars' incredible hopping ability at a hopping contest. *Below:* The spaceshiplike, double-engined *Invader* was built by famous car customizer George Barris.

The Amphicar

The Amphicar was one of the strangest production cars to come out of the 1960s. It doubled as a boat, allowing drivers to cruise on land and water. But in the end, the Amphicar did not sell well. Part of the reason was that its steel frame rusted too quickly in water. But the curious car remains very popular among collectors.

Hybrids

In recent years, cars that conserve fuel have become more and more popular. One solution is a hybrid car. This is a car that runs partly on gasoline and partly on batteries. Most major automakers have one or more hybrids on the market. Among the most popular is the Toyota Prius. This little car almost brings to mind the minicars of years past. But unlike those cars, the Prius and other hybrids are dependable and fully functional. Plus, most get more than 50 miles per gallon (21 km per liter), a big savings as well as helping the environment.

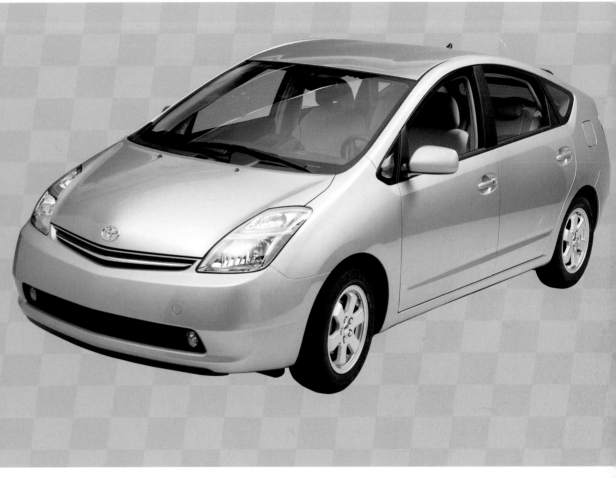

Built in France, the Flipper looked like the front half of a boat that had been chopped off at the middle. The Flipper didn't even have a reverse gear. Instead, the driver just turned the front wheels all the way around and drove backward.

In the 1980s and 1990s, the custom-car craze continued. There seemed to be no end to the creativity people put into their cars. Just as in the early days of the automobile, building cars that looked like animals remained popular. One driver turned his Ford Mustang convertible into a big hippopotamus. The car even had a tail that wagged.

Concept cars also grew more popular than ever. Automakers came up with some of the wackiest ideas yet. The Mercedes *F-300 Life Jet* was designed so the entire car leaned over in turns. The Isuzu *Como* looked like a combination of a car, a spaceship, and a pickup truck. The Oldsmobile

Toyota's smiling POD was designed to be more than just a car—it's a family friend.

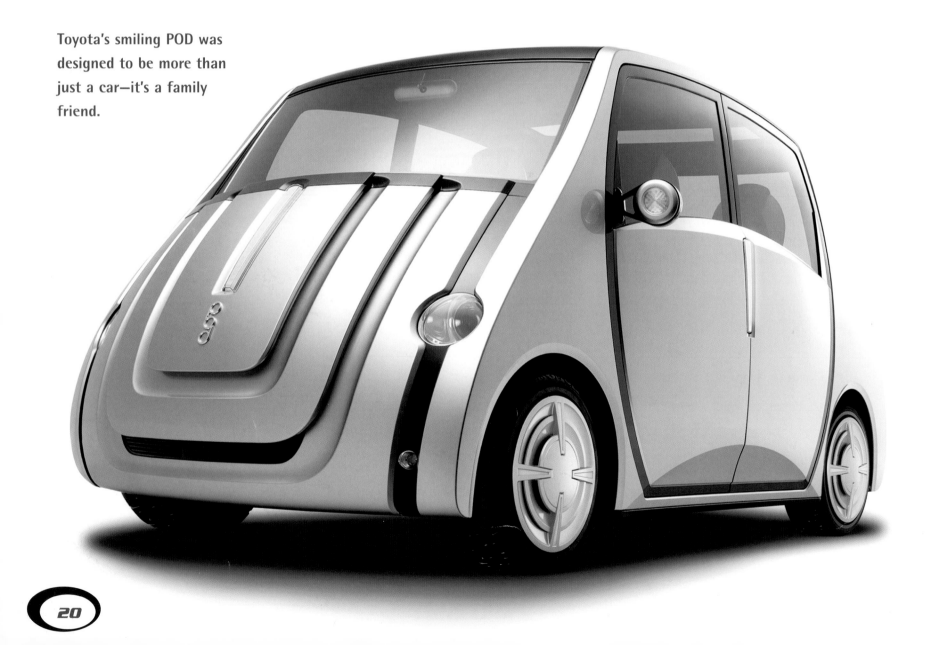

Aerotech was designed for pure speed. This experimental vehicle could go almost 280 miles (450 km) per hour.

Designers aren't holding back during the early 2000s. Modern concept cars are more than just new designs. Many of the new ideas change the way people think about what a car can be. Toyota built the POD (Personality On Demand), a tiny concept car, in the early 2000s. The POD works to build a relationship between a car and its driver. The car has a set of small lights that it uses to "talk" to the driver. Its electrical face can show 10 different emotions, including happiness and anger. Its rear antenna can even wag like a dog's tail. The POD doesn't stop there. It also learns a driver's musical preferences and even gives driving tips based on the driver's mood. The POD is just one example of how cars of the future may be even stranger than the crazy cars of the past.

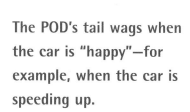

The POD's tail wags when the car is "happy"—for example, when the car is speeding up.

Chapter Two

CRAZY CAR CULTURE

The world of crazy cars is big and diverse. Crazy cars can be one-of-a-kind oddities, factory-made blunders, or unusual machines from the past. For every kind of crazy car in the world, there's someone who enjoys and appreciates it. Car lovers form clubs, gather at car shows, and take part in parades. Some clubs, such as the National Street Rod Association, have tens of thousands of members.

Others, such as the Amphicar Owners Club, are much smaller. Local car clubs meet almost anywhere—restaurants, city parks, or even unused parking lots. But all clubs, large or small, have one thing in common. The cars are always the center of attention.

Concept Cars

For decades, automakers have spent millions of dollars developing cars that

they never intend to sell. These concept cars are idea cars. They allow automakers to experiment with new shapes and ideas. Some of the results have been strange, futuristic designs.

The process of building a concept car is unique. In most cases, designers don't have to worry about mass production. Some don't even have engines or interiors. Most designers start by sketching a concept on paper. They draw the car from different angles. They focus on different parts. Next, they build a 3-D computer model of the car.

Before the car is built, it goes through one more stage—the clay

The GM AUTOnomy has an ambitious design. Each wheel is powered by a separate hydrogen-fuel-cell-powered engine. The car's body can be easily removed and exchanged for a different body type—a two-door coupe, a four-door sedan, etc.

Building a clay model is one of the most important stages of car design. The model allows the car to be viewed from all different angles. This model is being created by a student at the College for Creative Studies in California, one of the world's top automotive design schools.

model. The models are usually built at one-fifth scale (meaning all of the parts are one-fifth normal size). The model is carefully sculpted and painted. If an automaker likes the design, the car will be built. Unlike mass-production cars, much of a concept car is built by hand. Because most of them are one of a kind, normal assembly-line techniques won't work.

Finally, a concept car arrives at an auto show. In huge showrooms, automakers show off the new designs to the media and the public. Automakers make a grand show of unveiling each new concept, hoping to attract as much attention as possible. For visitors to an auto show, it's a chance to see new cars up close in a way they'd never be able to otherwise.

Lowriders and Art Cars

Lowriding is one of the most interesting car cultures. Every lowrider is unique and just a little bit crazy. Lowrider owners—who are also called lowriders—create cars that are works of art. Lowriders give their cars custom paint jobs. They use paint and a clear coating to give the cars a bright, shiny look. Many have special murals painted on the roof, hood, or door panels. Almost anything goes on a lowrider mural. Paintings may be of religious figures, famous people, cartoon characters, monsters, or anything else the owner can imagine.

Owners don't stop with the outside, though. They also customize the insides of their lowriders. They add plush interior fabric and carpet. Many owners add powerful sound systems with big speakers. Some add crazy accessories, such as televisions, window blinds, and even fish tanks.

Lowriders aren't just wild-looking cars. They are expressions of a person's artistic talent and skill. In the 1930s and 1940s, Mexican Americans

Lowriders are a way for car lovers to show off their creative skills. This lowrider is a heavily customized 1949 Buick Sedanette.

Gleaming chrome and many coats of shiny paint help lowriders to look cool.

living in southern California looked for ways to stand out from the crowd. One way to do this was to make their cars really low. At first, they put heavy objects in the trunks of their cars to weigh them down. Later, some people experimented with modifying their cars' suspension (the parts that connect the wheels to the car) to make the car lower. Finally, in the 1950s, a man named Ron Aguirre put a hydraulic system on his car. Aguirre's

system allowed him to raise and lower his car just by flipping some switches.

In time, hydraulics became the norm on lowriders. In the 2000s, nearly all lowriders have hydraulics. Clever craftpersons have built very powerful hydraulic systems that can make the cars hop, jump, and even dance.

Lowriders compete in dancing and hopping competitions at lowrider shows around the country. In addition to dancing and hopping events, the shows also feature contests for the best-looking lowriders. Lowrider shows are a lot of fun. They are a great example of car culture in action.

Most shows are organized by lowrider clubs. Club members get together often to check out one another's cars and to share tips about customizing. They cruise the streets in groups and are usually the organizers of lowrider shows. And all club members proudly display their club plaques on their cars. The culture of lowriding is big and only getting bigger.

Art cars are similar to lowriders in some ways. Art cars are all about looks. They use their cars as a way to express themselves. Art car clubs are a way for owners to enjoy their hobby together. And art car parades are familiar sights on city streets around the country.

TWO FACED
Double-ended cars are one popular customization. Car owners weld the front halves of two cars together, so that a nose faces in either direction. Most double-ended cars can only go in one direction. But some owners fix the steering so that the car can be driven either way!

Dan Lohaus of New York City turned his old pickup into a TV truck. Naturally, when he drives by, everyone tunes in.

Not all weird cars are rare. The Volkswagen Beetle, or Bug, is one of the most popular cars in the world. It's easy to spot because of its stout, round body. It was first built in 1938 under the name VW Type 1. The car was based on a sketch made by German dictator Adolf Hitler.

Solar Cars

Solar-powered cars are among the strangest cars you'll ever see. For years, people have dreamed of a car that can run on the power of sunlight. While such cars do exist, they're not yet practical for everyday use. They're small, light, and very fragile. They're not built to take the tough treatment many people give their cars.

Despite these drawbacks, designers at car companies, university students, and even high school students are constantly coming up with new solar car designs. The dark solar panel covered cars are very strange. Builders try different shapes, trying to keep the cars small and lightweight. At the same time, they try to maximize the cars' surface area. More panels mean more power, so designers have to get as many solar panels on the car as they can.

Productmobiles

Productmobiles have a simple purpose—advertising. Companies build cars in the shape of hot dogs, candy, toothpaste tubes, and more. Their purpose is to get attention for their products.

SPEEDY SUNRAYCER

In 1987 General Motors built its version of the solar car, called the *Sunraycer*. The *Sunraycer* won the first World Solar Challenge in Australia. It beat its closest competition by more than two days!

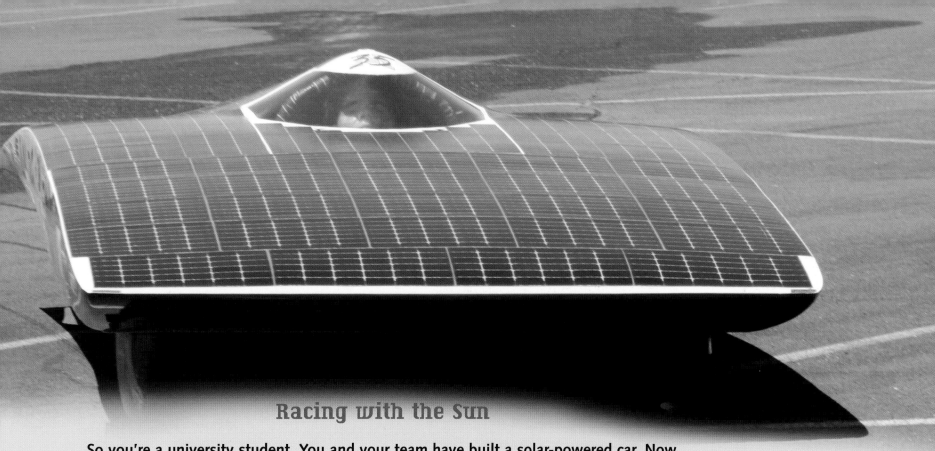

Racing with the Sun

So you're a university student. You and your team have built a solar-powered car. Now what do you do? Race it, of course! The North American Solar Challenge is a long-distance race designed to test the speed, efficiency, and endurance of solar-powered cars. The first race was held in 1990. The event was successful, and the race has since been held every other year. Stanford University, Northwestern University, the Massachusetts Institute of Technology, and many other schools have competed.

The 2005 race began in Austin, Texas, and finished in Calgary, Alberta, Canada. The winner was *Momentum*, a car built by a team from the University of Michigan. *Momentum* barely edged out the University of Minnesota entry, *Borealis III (above)* by a mere 11 minutes. *Momentum* managed an average speed of just over 46 miles (74 km) per hour. The results show some impressive progress compared to the average speed of the 1990 race winner. That year, the University of Michigan's *Sunrunner* averaged just less than 25 miles (40 km) per hour.

The companies send the cars to all kinds of events—from parades to fairs to sporting events. The goal is to stir up attention.

The Oscar Mayer Wienermobile has been the world's most famous product-mobile since it first appeared in 1936. Kraft Foods paid the General Body Company of Chicago, Illinois, $5,000 to build the first Wienermobile, which was 13 feet (4 meters) long. Throughout the years, the company has constantly improved the design. The current Wienermobile is 27 feet (8.2 m) long. It has all the features of a modern vehicle—from a big sound system to a Global Positioning System (GPS).

Many other companies have their own productmobiles. Hershey's has the Kissmobile™. The Goldfish Mobile, a big yellow goldfish, advertises Goldfish crackers. The

The Batmobile

Many people recognize the Batmobile *(right)*, a futuristic car from the *Batman* TV show of the 1960s. But most people don't know that the Batmobile is based on a concept car—the 1955 Lincoln Futura. The Futura was built in Italy by hand at a cost of $250,000. It had a double, clear-plastic canopied top and long, hooded headlights and tailfins. Customizer George Barris acquired the car, which he turned into the Batmobile for the 1960s TV show.

Tonymobile promotes Kellogg's cereals by featuring characters such as Tony the Tiger. Productmobiles don't just help sell food for people, though. The Meow Mix Mobile, shaped like a giant cat, advertises cat food. Other productmobiles help promote ideas. The Pfizer Revolution Mobile has a giant dog and cat and helps to educate people about their pets' health.

Weird Racing Cars

Some people live for the thrill of speed. Going fast—or making cars go fast— gets their hearts pumping. And the only thing more exciting than one fast car is a bunch of fast cars on the same track. With the quest for more and more speed, the world of racing has turned out some of the craziest cars around.

Cars that owners have specialized for different kinds of racing have taken on new and unusual forms. Top-fuel dragsters are among the craziest. These superpowerful cars are long and low. A drag race is just a quarter-mile (0.4-km) long, so acceleration is key. The cars can accelerate to more than 300 miles (480 km) per hour in only a few seconds. A tall airfoil, or wing, sits high above the dragster's rear. The airfoil works kind of like a backward airplane wing. Instead of using air pressure to lift, as a wing does, the airfoil pushes down on the car. It gives the wheels a better grip on the racing surface.

Funny cars are another kind of drag-racing vehicle. They look like normal cars. But their bodies are made of a one-piece shell. The shell easily flips up from the front to show the frame underneath. Funny cars also can reach speeds of more than 300 (480 km) miles per hour. Once they cross the finish line, drivers release parachutes from behind the cars to slow down.

Cars built for racing on oval tracks can also take on strange shapes. Open-wheel race cars—including Formula One cars, Champ cars, and stock cars—all have the same basic shape. They look like big go-karts. But while these cars may look like toys, they pack plenty of power. All can top speeds of more than 200 miles (320 km) per hour. Another type of open-wheel racer is the sprint car. These little cars have huge airfoils that sit high above them. They tear around small

Fire-breathing funny cars are some of the fastest—and loudest—machines on Earth.

dirt tracks, running almost sideways around most turns.

Regardless of which type of racing it is, race fans are among the most loyal sports fans in the world. They often go from track to track to support their favorite drivers. They plan their entire day—sometimes an entire weekend—around a race. From campouts to cookouts, race fans are there to watch and support the motor sports they love.

The past one hundred years have seen a wide variety of cars come and go. Some are remembered for their beauty, their speed, or their popularity. But a select group of cars are remembered for different reasons. They were the result of people thinking differently, trying new things—of being just a little bit crazy. In the 2000s, technology is growing and changing so quickly that it's exciting to think of what kind of crazy cars will come next.

The giant wing on the top of a sprint car works like an upside-down airplane wing. It creates downforce that pushes the car onto the track for better traction.

Philion Road Carriage (1892)

One of the oldest U.S.-built automobiles is the 1892 *Philion Road Carriage*. Circus performer Achille Philion started work on his invention in 1887. The car, which ran first on coal and later on oil, had a seat in front for the driver and one in back for a chauffeur. The chauffeur's job was to keep the engine working and producing the steam that powered the car.

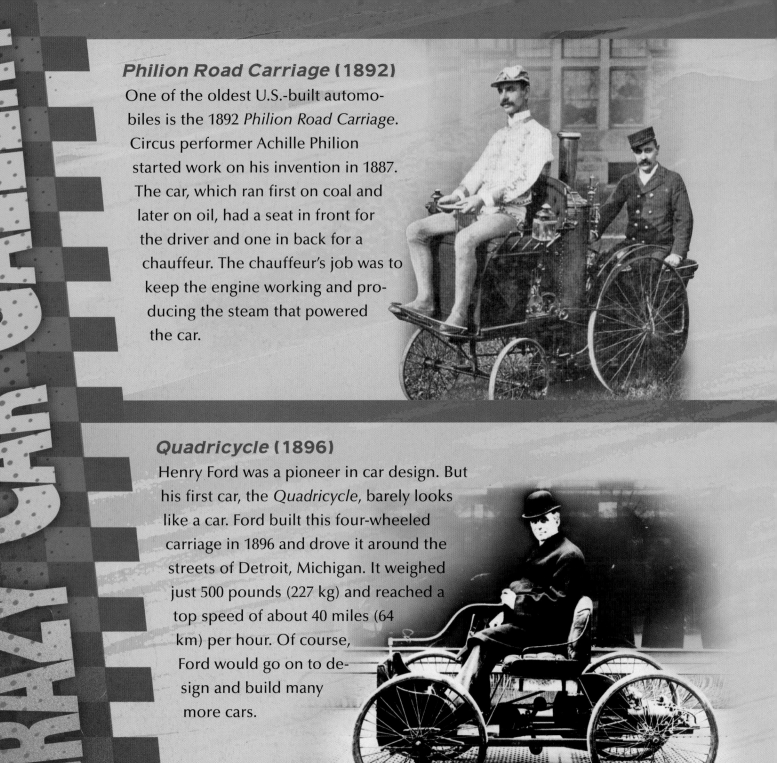

Quadricycle (1896)

Henry Ford was a pioneer in car design. But his first car, the *Quadricycle*, barely looks like a car. Ford built this four-wheeled carriage in 1896 and drove it around the streets of Detroit, Michigan. It weighed just 500 pounds (227 kg) and reached a top speed of about 40 miles (64 km) per hour. Of course, Ford would go on to design and build many more cars.

Octoauto (1910–1911)

Four wheels weren't enough for M. O. Reeves. Around 1910 he designed and built an eight-wheeled car called the Octoauto. He brought his invention to a 1911 car show in Chicago, Illinois, where it was a hit. But the car's extra wheels and long frame made it very expensive to build, so the Octoauto was never more than a curiosity. Reeves also built a six-wheeled car that he called the Sextoauto.

Dynasphere (1930s)

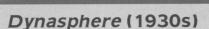

Since cars have been around, designers have played around with the number of wheels they have. In the early 1930s, a sketch by famous artist Leonardo da Vinci inspired British inventor Dr. John Purves. From da Vinci's idea, Purves created a one-wheeled car that he called the *Dynasphere*. The *Dynasphere's* driver sat in the middle of one giant wheel. While the car could move along just fine, it was almost impossible to steer or brake. Any hard braking actually sent the driver spinning head-over-heels inside the wheel. Not surprisingly, Purves's car never caught on.

Airomobile (1937)

Countless car designers have tried to make three-wheeled cars work. The teardrop-shaped *Airomobile* is one such attempt. The car's aerodynamic body style and low center of gravity allowed it to tear around corners at speeds much faster than the usual four-wheeled cars. But the design never took off. This model was the only one built.

Aerocar (1948)

The late 1940s were a golden age for both cars and airplanes. The end of World War II sparked big developments in both industries. So it's little surprise that a Longview, Washington, man named Molt Taylor decided to combine the two. Taylor's Aerocar, designed in 1948, made its first flight in 1956. It could go just 56 miles (90 km) per hour on the ground. But in the air, it could reach 125 miles (200 km) per hour.

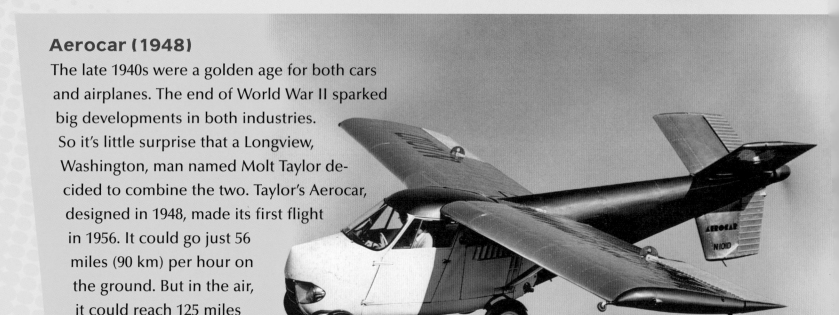

"Suede" Ford (1950)

Ford cars from this classic period are very popular with hot rodders. This car is painted flat (not shiny) black. The term *suede* comes from the flat paint. The paint is actually a primer, or undercoat paint. Early hot-rodders who couldn't afford to prime and paint their rides often just primed them. Before long, the flat look became popular. Whitewall tires and small, shiny hubcaps are other hallmarks of the suede look.

BMW Isetta (1953)

Gasoline was scarce in war-torn post-World War II Europe. The Isetta was BMW's answer to the demand for cheap, fuel-efficient transportation. Nicknamed the rolling egg, BMW's minicar had a small motorcycle engine that could power its light frame to 53 miles (85 km) per hour. The Isetta got more than 60 miles per gallon (26 km per liter) of fuel. The driver and passenger got in and out by opening the front of the car.

GM Firebird II (1956)

General Motors came out with one of the most memorable concept cars in 1956—the *Firebird II*. With its pointed nose and tailfin, the *Firebird II* looks as much like a spaceship as a car. The *Firebird II* is big enough to seat four. It has a body made of a space-age metal known as titanium. It also featured a 200-horsepower jet turbine engine. This GM car of the future was also supposed to have a special system that guided the car along highways, allowing the driver to rest.

Brütsch Mopetta (1958)

The Mopetta was designed to be the world's smallest car. With a tiny 3-cubic-inch (50-cubic-centimeter) engine and a light fiberglass body, the car could go about 21 miles (34 km) per hour. It was just 67 inches (170 cm) long and 34 inches (88 cm) wide. The Mopetta never took off commercially, though. Only 14 units were built.

Ford Nucleon (1958)

The designers of this 3/8-scale model concept car were looking far into the future. The Ford Nucleon was designed to be powered by a small nuclear reactor. (A nuclear reactor is a machine that produces energy by splitting atoms.) No real nuclear-powered cars have ever been built. Nuclear reactors are far too large and dangerous to put into a car. But the designers said that the Nucleon would be able to go 5,000 miles (8,047 km) before it needed recharging!

Chevrolet Impala Hearse (1959)

A hearse (funeral car) may seem like an odd choice for a lowrider, but no design is too crazy for some customizers. This 1959 Chevy Impala has a mean look to it, from the spikes on the front of the grille to the spooky tail end that some say looks like an angry Martian or a smiling cat. But this lowrider isn't just about looks. It also has a powerful supercharger sticking out of the hood. This car is slick, mean, and fast.

Beatnik Bandit (1960)

This wild, one-of-a-kind car was built by famous customizer Ed "Big Daddy" Roth. Inside the car's bubble top, the driver steered with a joystick instead of a steering wheel. The *Beatnik Bandit* was one of the first cars to be made into a Hot Wheels die-cast miniature. The Beatniks were members of a social movement of the late 1950s. The Beatniks tended to be young, artistic people who rejected normal American society. Like, crazy, man!

Amphicar (1961 – 1968)

The German-built Amphicar was a very clever idea. As a car, it reaches speeds of 65 miles per hour (105 km) on land. As a boat, it cruises at about 6 miles (10 km) per hour on water. Unfortunately, the Amphicar has a major design flaw. Its steel body rusts very quickly, so it can't spend too much time in the water. The quirky Amphicar remains very popular with collectors, however.

VW Beetle Lowrider (1970s)

The popular Volkswagen Beetle is a strange-looking car on its own. But when it's customized as a lowrider, it looks even crazier. This lowrider's bumpers have been removed, and the roof has been chopped off to give it an extra low look. Its doors open from the top down, while the trunk unhinges as a single piece.

De Lorean LK (1981)

The De Lorean sports coupe enjoyed a brief run of success in the 1980s. The popular sports car's most recognizable feature was its gull-wing doors that opened from the bottom up and looked like gulls' wings. The 1981 De Lorean pictured here was one of two cars plated in 24-karat gold. It was part of a promotion for American Express Gold credit card holders.

Kissmobile™ (1997)

It would be tough to miss the Hershey's Kissmobile™ rolling down the highway. The original Kissmobile™ was built in 1997 around a GMC truck. Three giant-sized models of the popular choco-late candy tower 12 feet (3.6 m) high. The driver sits in the furthest for-ward Kiss. The Kissmobile™ carries a big-screen TV, a karaoke sound sys-tem, and space to carry more than 230,000 Hershey's Kisses. Yum!

The Spammobile™ (2001)

You can smell this car coming a mile away. The Spammobile™ is equipped with electric grills for cooking miniature Spamburgers® to serve to a hungry public at concerts, sporting events, and other activities. The first Spammobile™ was built in 2001. Two more have followed, bringing the Spam™ fleet up to three. In total, the three trucks serve about 1.5 million sandwiches a year.

Chocolate VW Beetle (2003)

Not all crazy cars are built to last. In 2003 a shopping center in Japan coated a Volkswagen Beetle with almost 40 gallons (150 liters) of chocolate as part of a Valentine's Day promotion. That's one sweet ride!

Rinspeed Splash (2004)

A newer, more practical combination of boat and car is the Rinspeed Splash. The Swiss-built Splash can turn from a car into a boat at the push of a button. And if that's not enough, the Splash practically flies above the waves. A system of hydrofoils (skilike attachments) allows the car's hull to hover about 2 feet (0.6 m) above the water's surface.

Borealis III (2005)

Long, thin, and low, the *Borealis III* is built to run on the power of the sun. Students at the University of Minnesota built the car. It finished second at the 2005 North American Solar Challenge. The car's most noticeable feature is its large number of solar panels. They soak up the sun's rays and turn them into power. There's no need to stop at the gas station with this car!

Nissan Pivo (2005)

At less than 9 feet (2.7 m) long, the Pivo looks more like a toy than a real car. The Pivo's cabin, which seats three, can rotate all the way around. Drivers don't have to shift into reverse. They can just turn the cabin to go in the direction they want! The Pivo is equipped with a small but powerful electric motor.

Peugeot Moovie (2005)

The Moovie is what you get when you hold a contest for the best futuristic car design. That's exactly what the automaker Peugeot did. Portuguese designer André Costa took the prize. His Moovie is a two-seat electric car. The two rear wheels are so large that the car's doors are actually inside them. The car's steering wheel doesn't even move the wheels. Instead, the car turns by making one wheel go faster than the other.

Top-Fuel Dragster (2006)

Long, thin top-fuel dragsters aren't just among the world's fastest cars, they're also among the most bizarre. Also called rails, these cars can accelerate to more than 300 miles (483 km) per hour in just seconds. Their powerful supercharged engines burn a special high-powered fuel called nitromethane (nitro).

Glossary

concept car: an idea car built by automakers to test new ideas and to gain publicity

customize: to change a vehicle's appearance

horseless carriage: the name given to the earliest automobiles

hot rod: a type of car customized for both looks and speed

hybrid: a car that runs partly on gasoline and partly on electricity

hydraulics: a system of pumps that lift heavy objects

lowrider: a custom car built with hydraulics and designed to run low to the ground

minicar: a tiny car, often having only three wheels and an electric motor

mural: a themed painting on a lowrider

productmobile: a vehicle built to look like a product

propeller: a set of spinning blades that gives power to vehicles such as airplanes and boats

Selected Bibliography

Genat, Robert. *Lowriders*. Saint Paul: Motorbooks International, 2003.

Gunnell, John A. *Weird Cars*. Iola, WI: Krause Publications, 1993.

Rees, Chris. *Concept Cars: An A-Z Guide to the World's Most Fabulous Futuristic Cars*. New York: Barnes & Noble Books, 2000.

Vokins, Stephen. *Weird Cars: A Century of the World's Strangest Cars*. Newbury Park, CA: J. H. Haynes & Co., 2004.

Further Reading

Abraham, Philip. *Cars*. New York: Children's Press, 2004.

Braun, Eric. *Hot Rods*. Minneapolis: Lerner Publications Company, 2007.

Doeden, Matt. *Lowriders*. Minneapolis: Lerner Publications Company, 2007.

Maurer, Tracy. *Lowriders*. Vero Beach, FL: Rourke Publishing, 2004.

Piehl, Janet. *Formula One Race Cars*. Minneapolis: Lerner Publications Company, 2007.

Simon, Seymour. *Cool Cars*. New York: Seastar Books, 2003.

Zuehlke, Jeffrey. *Concept Cars*. Minneapolis: Lerner Publications Company, 2007.

Websites

American Solar Challenge
http://www.americansolarchallenge.org
This is the homepage of the North American Solar Challenge, a solar car race held each summer. The site includes news, photos, and information about the cars in the race.

The Car Connection
http://www.thecarconnection.com
Offers news, reviews, and photos of new cars.

Strange Cars Zone
http://www.autozine.org/strange_car/strange_menu.htm
Autozine.com's page devoted to strange cars features almost 30 weird cars, with photos and descriptions.

The Wienermobile
http://www.kraftfoods.com/om/Wienermobile_main.htm
The home page of the Oscar Mayer Wienermobile includes a detailed history of the most famous productmobile and its many designs.

Index

About the Author

Matt Doeden is a freelance author and editor living in Minnesota. He's written more than 50 children's books, including dozens on cars and drivers.

About the Consutant

Jan Lahtonen is a safety engineer, auto mechanic, and lifelong automobile enthusiast.

Photo Acknowledgments

© Getty Images, pp. 4–5, 6 (top background and bottom), 7, 9, 11 (both), 31, 34 (bottom), 35 (bottom), 38 (bottom), 44 (bottom), 45 (bottom); Photo Courtesy of National Automobile Museum (The Harrah Collection), pp. 8, 34 (top), 36 (top), 40 (top), 41 (bottom); GEORGE EASTMAN HOUSE, pp. 10, 35 (top); © Jim Lightfoot, p. 12; Copyright 2006 GM Corp. Used with permission, GM Media Archive, pp. 13, 22, 23; © Hulton-Deutsch Collection/CORBIS, p. 14; © Ralph Crane/Time Life Pictures/Getty Images, p. 15 (top); © CORBIS, pp. 15 (bottom), 36 (bottom); © Bettmann/CORBIS, pp. 16 (both), 28, 37 (bottom), 38 (top), 39 (top); © Ted Soqui/CORBIS, pp. 17 (top), 26; © Mike Key, pp. 17 (bottom), 25, 37 (top), 39 (bottom), 41 (top); © Philippe Caron/Sygma/CORBIS, pp. 18, 40 (bottom); © Toyota Motor Sales, U.S.A., Inc., p. 19; © Toyota Motor Corporation, pp. 20, 21; College for Creative Studies, p. 24; TV truck by Dan Lohaus, Photo © Harrod Blank www.artcaragency.com, p. 27; © Todd Strand/Independent Picture Service, pp. 29, 44 (top); © Jeffrey Zuehlke, pp. 30, 42 (top); © David Allio/Icon SMI/CORBIS, p.32; © Artemis Images/Pikes Peak International Hill Climb, p. 33; Photo Courtesy of Hormel Foods Corporation, p. 42 (bottom); © Hironori Miyata/Camera Press/Retna Ltd., p. 43 (top); Rinspeed Inc., p. 43 (bottom); © Boris Roessler/epa/CORBIS, p. 45 (top).

Front Cover: Photo © Harrod Blank www.artcaragency.com.